Herald Press
Meditation Books

By Helen Good Brenneman
Meditations for the Expectant Mother
Meditations for the New Mother

By John M. Drescher
Meditations for the Newly Married

By Vernell Klassen Miller
Meditations for Adoptive Parents

By Larry Wilson
Daily Fellowship with God

By Various Authors
Visitation Pamphlet Series

Meditations for
the New Mother

" He gathers the lambs in his arms and
carries them close to his heart;
he gently leads those that have young."
Isaiah 40:11b

Meditations for the New Mother

Revised Edition

HELEN GOOD BRENNEMAN

Drawings by
ESTHER ROSE GRABER

A devotional book for
the new mother during the first
month following the birth
of her baby

HERALD PRESS
Scottdale, Pennsylvania
Waterloo, Ontario

The paper used in this publication is recycled and meets
the minimum requirements of American National Standard
for Information Sciences—Permanence of Paper for
Printed Library Materials, ANSI Z39.48-1984.

Unless otherwise indicated, Bible quotations are from *Holy Bible,
New International Version* ®, copyright © 1973, 1978, 1984 by
International Bible Society. Used by permission of Zondervan
Publishing House. All rights reserved

MEDITATIONS FOR THE NEW MOTHER

Copyright © 1953, 1981, 1985 by Herald Press,
Scottdale, Pa. 15683
   Published simultaneously in Canada by Herald Press,
   Waterloo, Ont. N2L 6H7. All rights reserved
Library of Congress Catalog Card Number: 85-71141
International Standard Book Numbers:
   0-8361-3399-4 (softcover)
   0-8361-3400-1 (hardcover)
Printed in the United States of America

Forty-sixth printing 1995
500,500 copies in print

To my own dear mother
who first revealed to me
the beauty of motherhood

Author's Preface

Today you are a *mother*. Beside you lies a little person, wrapped in the swaddling clothes of innocency, purity, love, and trust. How you deserve this child, you will never fully understand. What lies in store for the newborn, only the future will reveal. This new life will survive the ages, and is even now a part of things eternal, for Jesus said, "Of such is the kingdom of heaven."

All in all, you have had a momentous experience, and joy has been written into every chapter of it. There was personal joy, an unequaled thrill over the baby's first cry. There was family joy, for the coming of the new member draws parents closer together than ever before. There was spiritual joy, for you have cooperated with God your Maker in the wonderful creation of a new life.

Great moments in one's life are never without their special problems, though, and certainly new motherhood has its full share. You may have thought that you had fully prepared for the coming of the little basket-dweller, but there are many details which now require your constant attention. The human infant is the most helpless of all God's babies, and all the answers are not to be found in the baby book!

Doctors will tell you that while your strength is coming back, physical and glandular changes are taking place in your body which can affect your emotional life. And since one's spiritual life is so closely associated with one's physical and emotional well-being, you no doubt feel the need of the loving presence of God in a very special way at this time.

As a result of my own experience of new motherhood, with its accompanying joys and problems, I have prepared this book of *Meditations for the New Mother*, a collection of Scriptures, poetry, and devotional thoughts especially meaningful after the birth of a baby. My prayer is that the rich passages of the Word of God will not only inspire you during that first important month of your baby's life, but will continue to guide you in your lifelong task of motherhood.

I wish to thank especially Mary Royer, Ph.D., Goshen College, Goshen, Indiana, and my husband, Virgil Brenneman, as well as many other friends for their kind help and encouragement in the completion of this book.

Helen Good Brenneman

Contents

OUR RESPONSIBILITY TO THE CHILD

Thanksgiving for the Child

"I prayed for this child."
1 Samuel 1:27

"I prayed for this child, and the Lord has granted me what I asked of him. So now I give him to the Lord. For his whole life he will be given over to the Lord."

1 Samuel 1:27, 28

The Fruit of Your Womb

"Lo, children are an heritage of the Lord:
    And the fruit of the womb is his reward.
As arrows are in the hand of a mighty man;
    So are children of the youth.
Happy is the man that hath his quiver full of them."
                                            Psalm 127:3-5a, KJV

At the dawn of the world, in the morning of time, God looked down upon the beautiful earth which he had made and climaxed creation by placing a man and a woman in the first home. Life together for the world's first married couple must have been romantic and very happy, for they knew love and wholeness, and their garden-home was exquisitely furnished.

Yet God, in wisdom, knew that two young people, however much in love, needed something to lift them above themselves and make their affection of a deeper, more lasting nature. Indeed, so great had been God's satisfaction in creating this young couple that, wishing to share creative joy, he commanded them to be fruitful, to multiply, and to replenish the earth.

Thus began family life on the earth. Bearing and bringing up children has continued throughout the ages to be a tender and joyful experience. Thus it was ages later when Solomon, king and father, wrote of the happiness that comes with children, the heritage of God. Thus it was that Jesus personally took the babies of his day into his arms to bless them. And thus it is for *you*, to-day, New Mother, as you join hands with the mothers of the ages, praising God your Maker for the fruit of your womb, your reward and heritage, your new baby!

Dear God, I thank you with all my heart for the beautiful experience of motherhood and for the infant at my side. Just as you have helped the mothers of all ages, guide me in my new task, bless my precious baby, and bless the baby's father in his love and concern for both of us. Amen.

A MOTHER

God sought to give the sweetest thing
  In his almighty power
To earth; and deeply pondering
  What it should be, one hour
In fondest joy and love of heart
  Outweighing every other,
He moved the gates of heaven apart
  And gave to earth a mother.

Author Unknown

A babe in a house is a wellspring of pleasure.

M. F. Topper

Hannah's Song

"Then Hannah prayed and said:
'My heart rejoices in the Lord. . . .
There is no one holy like the Lord;
there is no one besides you;
there is no Rock like our God.' "
1 Samuel 2:1a, 2

Read 1 Samuel 2:1-10.

Truly the story of Hannah is a woman's story; it is a mother's story. Our hearts beat sympathetically with the heart of this would-be mother who so much desired a child that "she wept and would not eat." Can you not see her at the temple as "in bitterness of soul" she cried out to God in prayer?

None of us who have felt that God-given hunger for motherhood and for the warmth of a baby in our arms would censure her for the agreement which she made with God. Neither did God reprove her, but answered her prayer, accepted her child, and used him mightily in his kingdom. And then, to end the story beautifully, God gave her three more sons and two daughters to bless her life and to fill her home with joy.

Little Samuel was a *wanted* child and his earliest years were filled with his mother's love. Moreover, Hannah did not forget God when her prayer was answered, as so many do today. When her child was weaned, she took him to the temple, gave him to the Lord, and uttered a prayer that has come down to us through the ages. The prayer expresses joy in her God, victory over her difficulties, stability founded upon the rock of her salvation, humility, strength, and justice.

Let us today follow Hannah's example as we, too, "give thanks to the Lord for his unfailing love and his wonderful deeds."

O Lord, my refuge and my fortress, my rock, in whom I trust, I praise you for the protection of your wings and for the strength of your presence. I thank you also for laying this little child in my arms to love and to cherish. Help me, as mother, always to dwell under the shadow of the Almighty, in the secret place of the Most High. Amen.

17

HIS CRADLE

It rocked and rocked for joy,
  This battered world,
When Mary's little boy
  Up in it curled,
    Despite its chill.
    O may he fill
Today his chosen bed,
  Through you and me,
Who love and help to spread
  Simplicity.

Herbert Seymour Hastings

The Birth of Our Lord

"But the angel said to her,
   'Do not be afraid, Mary, you have found favor with God.
   You will be with child and give birth to a son,
   and you are to give him the name Jesus. . . .'
And she gave birth to her firstborn, a son.
   She wrapped him in strips of cloth
   and placed him in a manger."

Luke 1:30-31 and 2:7a

Read Luke 2:1-7.

How strange it seems to us, as we lie in our comfortable beds, that the Lord of glory, who deserved the most luxurious cradle in all the world, should be born in a barn and cushion his downy head on a pillow of straw! How bumpy the ride must have seemed to Mary as she traveled, probably on the back of a donkey, all the way from Nazareth to Bethlehem! She may even have walked those hundred miles. Did she and Joseph understand the prophecy concerning Jesus' birthplace, or did they sometimes fear that the child might be born before they reached their destination?

A little girl, in a well-to-do home, said one day, "Mamma, I don't understand why, if God is so rich, he let his Son be born in a manger. Why didn't he buy him a little bed like mine?"

We could speculate on the delivery in that unsanitary stable, the lack of an attendant physician, the simple layette which Mary had brought along from her home. But all these details are lost in the splendor of the occasion, beginning when the angel first told Mary that she was to bring forth the "Son of the Most High." The simplicity of the setting accentuates the beauty of the child, the wonder of his coming, and the quiet worship of the first visitors who knelt at his feet.

May we at this joyous time of our lives meditate on the birth of our Savior, opening our hearts to him as never before!

God in heaven, who sent your Son to us as a little baby, I thank you for the miracle of birth. I thank you, too, that because a Savior was born into this world, I can be "born again" into the kingdom of God. May the birth of my child remind me of your Son who came that I, believing on him, might have life everlasting. Amen.

19

MATERNITY

Within the crib that stands beside my bed
A little form in sweet abandon lies
And as I bend above with misty eyes
I know how Mary's heart was comforted.

O world of Mothers! blest are we who know
The ecstasy—the deep God-given thrill
That Mary felt when all the earth was still
In that Judean starlight long ago!

Anne P. L. Field

Mary's Song

"And Mary said:
'My soul praises the Lord
and my spirit rejoices in God my Savior,
for he has been mindful of the humble state of his servant.
From now on all generations will call me blessed.' "

Luke 1:46-48

Read Luke 1:46-55.

When expectant mothers get together, there is always a great deal of hopeful, animated conversation. But the famous meeting of Mary, the mother of Jesus, and Elizabeth, the mother of John the Baptist, had more than the usual amount of excitement and joy. Filled with the Spirit, Elizabeth shouted,

"Blessed are you among women,
And blessed is your child! . . .
For as soon as your greeting reached my ears,
The baby leaped for joy within me!" (Williams Translation)

Mary's Magnificat of thanksgiving is much like the song of Hannah. Mary, too, makes the occasion one of praise for God's greatness, holiness, mercy, strength, and justice. In her gratitude she wonders at the Almighty's choice of a peasant girl, such as herself, to be forever blessed among women.

If Mary's heart were so filled with praise before Jesus was born, can you imagine her joy when at last God Incarnate lay in her arms as a tiny babe? After the shepherds had returned to their fields, Luke tells us that "Mary treasured up all these things and pondered them in her heart." Hers must have been an unassuming, devout personality, as she meditated upon the momentous events of her days, looking to God for strength to face her new responsibilities.

Our task is second only to Mary's, and the God of our strength is the same loving Friend who watched over the divine infant two thousand years ago. Let us, like Mary, face the future with praise, confidence, and unconquerable faith in our God.

My Friend and my God, my heart has thrilled over the praise and thanksgiving of Mary, Jesus' mother. I cannot find words to express my joy as she did, but you know what is in my heart. I give you my heartfelt thanks and ask of you courage for the days and nights ahead. Amen.

COMETH THE CHILD

Fresh from the hand of the Father,
New from his latest creating,
Clean from Love's all-golden weather
To a bleak climate of hating,
To the old failures of ages,
To a worn book, a stale story
Onto earth's intricate pages
Cometh the child in his glory.

Through him our purpose, once restive,
Focuses full upon duty;
Through him our joy gains refining,
We through his eyes see new beauty.
Through him our haughty hearts crumble,
The hills and the vales are made even;
Through him our proud souls made simple
Find grace at the threshold of heaven.

Miriam Sieber Lind

Elizabeth's Preparation

"Both of them were upright in the sight of God,
observing all the Lord's commandments and
regulations blamelessly."
Luke 1:6

Read Luke 1:5-17.

God, who sees not as we see, but looks on the heart, did not choose men and women of great worldly influence to take part in the events surrounding the birth of our Savior. Instead God selected poor, humble, ordinary folks, people who were "observing all the Lord's commandments and regulations blamelessly." And what better qualification for parenthood can we find than a pious, God-fearing heart such as God saw in Zechariah and Elizabeth?

Some of the account of the birth of John the Baptist describes the experiences of Zechariah, his initial struggle with doubt, and his final triumph of faith. But of Elizabeth we read of her joy that the Lord had finally taken away her barrenness in answer to her prayer. We see her faith, her receptiveness, and her obedience in the naming and training of her son. What a commentary on her character, that the angel Gabriel could send the youthful Mary to Elizabeth to be strengthened in courage and in faith!

Because of her faithfulness, Elizabeth was able to carry out the plan which God had for her, and her son "continued to grow and to gain strength in the Spirit" (Luke 1:80, Williams).

Although the purpose of the little life at our side has not been announced to us by angels, God just as surely has a plan for this new life as he did for that of John the Baptist. Thus our song of thanksgiving should be accompanied by a prayer for inward purity, that we, too, may be prepared to carry out God's will in the training of our child.

I see, dear God, that the most important preparation for me in my duties as a mother is to live a righteous life of integrity as an example to my child. Since I cannot do this in my own strength, come into my heart and live there. Strengthen my inner self with the presence of your Spirit. In Jesus' name I ask this. Amen.

ON PARENTING

They say that man is mighty,
He governs land and sea,
He wields a mighty scepter
O'er lesser powers than he;

But mightier power and stronger
Man from his throne has hurled,
For the hand that rocks the cradle
Is the hand that rules the world.

W. R. Wallace

An ounce of mother is worth a pound of clergy.

Spanish Proverb

Jochebed's Privilege

"And she became pregnant and gave birth to a son. When she saw that he was a fine child, she hid him for three months. But when she could hide him no longer, she got a papyrus basket for him and . . . placed the child in it and put it among the reeds along the bank of the Nile."

Exodus 2:2, 3

Read Exodus 2:1-10.

Little Moses was born in troublesome times, in an age when Hebrew mothers rightly felt insecure about the future of their infant sons. So intent was Pharaoh on subduing the Jewish people, that he used every horrible method in his power to halt the increase of this minority group in his land.

We do not know much about Jochebed, Moses' mother, but she must have been endowed with a generous portion of motherly wisdom and guided by a higher power. For she carried out a plan which not only saved the life of her baby, but established him in the palace of the monarch who sought to destroy him.

When Moses was born, his mother was probably too busy keeping him hidden from the authorities to write a song of thanksgiving such as Hannah and Elizabeth did. But when he was three months old, how she must have rejoiced! God, in providence, had given her the privilege of caring for her son and training him in ways of righteousness for a lifetime of service. Although Jochebed did not know it then, her little son would one day become a great leader of God's people.

Certainly God is honored by our words of praise and thanksgiving, but wants something more of us. God wants us to show our gratitude by bringing up sons and daughters who, like Moses, "refused to be known as the son of Pharaoh's daughter. He chose to be mistreated along with the people of God rather than to enjoy the pleasures of sin for a short time" (Hebrews 11:24-25).

Gracious God, I thank you for the example of Jochebed, one of the great mothers of all time. If you could deliver her from such great danger, certainly you can also guide me in the perplexing problems of caring for my baby. For I, too, want to take good care of my child and nurture this little one for service. Amen.

25

THE NEW BABY

"How funny and red!"
That's what they said.
"Why, there's nothing but fuzz
On top of his head."
And they lifted the covers
To look at his feet.
"Oh, how tiny and wrinkled
And red as a beet!"
And I heard them whispering
Behind my back,
"Did you ever think
He would look like that,
All wrinkled and red
Like a baby bird?"
Of course they didn't
Know that I heard.
But I had to smile
When the baby was fed
To see how fast
They lined up by his bed,
And in spite of the fact
He was wrinkled and thin,
They begged for a turn
At holding him.

Osie Hertzler Ziegler

26

Family Joy

"God sets the lonely in families."
Psalm 68:6

"Your wife will be like a fruitful vine
within your house;
your [children] will be like olive shoots
around your table."
Psalm 128:3

In a day when family life is disintegrating, when selfishness breaks up homes and brings unwanted children into the world, how refreshing and how stabilizing is our never-changing God who is ever present in the Christian home!

According to Psalm 128, it is the man that fears the Lord, who walks in his ways, who finds in his wife and children the deepest and finest satisfaction. Psalm 127 says, "Blessed is the man whose quiver is full of them [children]." Of course, the "quiverful" joy of which the psalmist speaks is not selfish parental pride, which takes personal glory for a God-given gift. While "quiverful" joy does not express itself in boasting about one's children, it does bring with it, however, a wholesome type of self-respect, as well as respect in the community.

The woman who receives and responds to a call from God to motherhood is acting in accordance with the plan of an all-knowing God for her life. The psalmist pictures her here as a beautiful, fruitful vine, and the writer of the Proverbs says that her value is far above rubies. In motherhood, as in all areas of life, living in the will of God brings inner peace, delightful experiences, and lasting satisfaction in addition to the daily round of problems, trials, and hard-learned lessons.

Dear Parent of fathers and mothers, I thank you for establishing the home as a place where we can share life's most beautiful relationships. I thank you for making me a woman, a wife, and a mother. May I be worthy of this call; may I make my home a joyous place. In Jesus' name. Amen.

A NEW LIFE

A tired old doctor died today, and a baby boy was born—
A little new soul that was pink and frail,
    and a soul that was gray and worn.
And—halfway here and halfway there
On a white, high hill of shining air—
They met and passed and paused to speak
    in the flushed and hearty dawn.

The man looked down at the soft, small thing,
    with wise and weary eyes;
And the little chap stared back at him,
    with startled, scared surmise,
And then he shook his downy head—
"I think I won't be born," he said;
"You are too gray and sad!" And he shrank
    from the pathway down the skies.

But the tired old doctor roused once more
    at the battle-cry of birth,
And there was memory in his look, of grief
    and toil and mirth.
"Go on!" he said. "It's good—and bad:
It's hard! Go on! It's ours, my lad."
And he stood and urged him out of sight,
    down to the waiting earth.

Harold Francis Branch

An Even Greater Joy

"A woman giving birth to a child has pain because her time has come; but when her baby is born she forgets the anguish because of her joy that a child is born into the world. So with you: Now is your time of grief, but I will see you again and you will rejoice, and no one will take away your joy."

John 16:21-22

These comforting words, which break forth with fresh meaning to the mother of a newborn baby, were spoken by Jesus to the bewildered disciples, shortly before his crucifixion. With this vivid illustration Jesus showed how the difficulties of true Christian discipleship will one day be swallowed up in everlasting happiness.

They sat dejected around their Master, those eleven disciples, wishing that he would assure them of a continuing special relationship, instead of talking about leaving for some faraway place. If only he would speak to them more plainly! They could not understand what he meant by, "In a little while you will see me no more, and then after a little while you will see me." The strange mixture of sorrow and joy, of suffering and comfort, of trouble and peace puzzled them deeply.

Not until after Jesus rose from the grave, went up into heaven, and poured out the Holy Spirit did the disciples fully understand, "In this world you will have trouble. But take heart! I have overcome the world." The Comforter *did* come and Jesus' prayer for the faithful followers was answered with spiritual power that continued bearing fruit through the centuries.

Bringing the lesson back to us, we have already forgotten those anxious hours of birthing, in the tremendous satisfaction that baby is here. How much more quickly we will forget life's problems when eternity suddenly ushers us into the long-awaited presence of our Lord Jesus Christ!

O Christ, I thank you for explaining the great truths of the kingdom in words I can understand. I thank you for earthly joys that remind me of the eternal pleasures with you. May I, today, sit in heavenly places with you, that in ages to come I may enjoy the exceeding riches of your grace in heaven itself. In your name I pray. Amen.

A TRIBUTE TO CHILDHOOD

When God made the child he began early in the morning. He watched the golden hues of the rising day chasing away the darkness, and he chose the azure of the opening heavens for the color of childhood's eyes, the crimson of the clouds to paint its cheeks, and the gold of the morning for its flowing tresses. He listened to the song of the birds as they sang and warbled and whispered, and strung childhood's harp with notes now soft and low—now sweet and strong.

He saw little lambs among the flock romp and play and skip, and put play into childhood's heart. He saw the silvery brook and listened to its music and he made the laughter of the child like the ripple of the brook. He saw angels of light as upon the wings of love they hastened to holy duty, and he formed the child's heart in purity and love.

And having made the child, he sent it out to bring joy into the home, laughter on the green, and gladness everywhere. He sent it into the home and said to the parents, "Nourish and bring up this child for me." He sent it to the church and said, "Teach it my love and my laws." He sent it to the state and said, "Deal tenderly with it and it will bless and not curse you." He sent it to the nation and said, "Be good to the child. It is thy greatest asset and thy hope."

George W. Rideout

The Perfect Gift

"Every good and perfect gift is from above, coming down from the Father of the heavenly lights, who does not change like shifting shadows. He chose to give us birth through the word of truth, that we might be a kind of firstfruits of all he created."

James 1:17-18

A friend of ours, charmed by the joys of first parenthood, wrote us in a letter, "I still wonder at what age parents may begin to take credit for such good behavior; so far the goodness of the gift reflects the greater goodness of the Giver." We all agree that there is no age when *we* can take credit for the miracle of love which is now ours, for the gift is absolutely unmerited and the glory belongs to the King of glory!

Our own wiggly little bundle came at Christmastime, reminding us in a special way that babies are remarkable gifts. Certainly no gift had ever brought with it such demands upon our time, energy, and pocketbook. But neither had any previous Christmas present brought eternal significance.

A divinely planned blend of both our personalities, our baby was at the same time a new and living soul. Scarcely aware of anything beyond personal needs, our child possesses an amazing capacity for love. This love develops and matures as our baby experiences the love of others and learns about the love of God.

And most significant of all, this gift was created by God in God's own image and for divine glory. Ours for today, this precious child is God's for eternity.

"How can I repay the Lord
    for all his goodness to me?
I will lift up the cup of salvation
    and call on the name of the Lord.
I will fulfill my vows to the Lord
    in the presence of all his people."

Psalm 116:12-14

THE MOTHER'S HYMN

Lord who ordainest for mankind
Benignant toils and tender cares,
We thank thee for the ties that bind
The mother to the child she bears.

We thank thee for the hopes that rise
Within her heart, as, day by day,
The dawning soul, from those young eyes,
Looks with a clearer, steadier ray.

And grateful for the blessing given
With that dear infant on her knee,
She trains the eye to look to heaven,
The voice to lisp a prayer to thee.

Such thanks the blessed Mary gave
When from her lap the Holy Child,
Sent from on high to seek and save
The lost of earth, looked up and smiled.

All-Gracious! grant to those who bear
A mother's charge, the strength and light
To guide the feet that own their care
In ways of Love and Truth and Right.

William Cullen Bryant

A Psalm of Thanksgiving

"Shout for joy to the Lord, all the earth.
Serve the Lord with gladness;
come before him with joyful songs.
Know that the Lord is God.
It is he who made us, and we are his;
we are his people, the sheep of his pasture.

"Enter his gates with thanksgiving
and his courts with praise;
give thanks to him and praise his name.
For the Lord is good and his love endures forever;
his faithfulness continues through all generations."

Psalm 100

Meditations on the Child

"The Lord has granted me what I asked."
1 Samuel 1:27

TO A CHILD I KNOW

Dear little child with eyes
Like violets glowing,
And face all dimpled with
Enchanting smile,
You have a beauty which is
Innocently flowing
Unhindered yet by any
Thought of guile.
Your soul is breathing
Peaceful as a flower,
And loving me keeps me
In touch with love,
Before the world steps in
I prize each precious hour,
That lifts my soul through you
To God above.

J. M. Ballantyne

As a Little Child

"A little child will lead them." **Isaiah 11:6**

"From the lips of children and infants you have ordained praise."
Matthew 21:16

"He took a little child and had him stand among them."
Mark 9:36

To Jesus' most intimate earthly friends, the twelve disciples, some of his words and actions were surely hard to understand. Although he was the greatest person who ever lived, the Son of the Highest, he told them that he had not come to save his life but to lose it. He came as a servant, not to be served but to serve.

Not long after Jesus said, "If anyone would come after me, he must deny himself," these poor, human disciples got into a foolish argument.

"I think *I* will be the greatest in the kingdom of heaven," was in essence what each one declared, giving no doubt his own convincing reasons.

How discouraging to the Lord Jesus, who had been trying to help them see what the *real* kingdom of God was like! But he did not rebuke them harshly. "If anyone wants to be first, he must be the very last, and the servant of all" (Mark 9:35).

Then Jesus gave them an object lesson they were not soon to forget. Drawing a little child into his arms, he told them that if they were to enter the kingdom *at all*, they would have to become as little children. And if they were to become truly great, they must be willing to treat even little children as they would treat him, their Lord.

It is easy to criticize those early followers, but how often we, too, are *childish* rather than *childlike*. How grateful we can be that God has set our little child in *our* midst, to demonstrate the simple virtues of innocence, meekness, trust, forgiveness, and love.

O Lord, you search me and know me. You know that many times I am not childlike in spirit, but childish and selfish. Teach me, by observing my own small baby, some of the spiritual qualities you would have me possess. Amen.

"Suffer that little children come to me,
Forbid them not." Emboldened by his words,
The mothers onward press; but, finding vain
The attempt to reach the Lord, they trust their babe
To strangers' hands; the innocents, alarmed
Amid the throng of faces all unknown,
Shrink, trembling, till their wandering eyes discern
The countenance of Jesus, beaming love
And pity; eager then they stretch their arms,
And, cowering, lay their heads upon his breast.

James Grahame

The Child and the Christ

" 'Let the little children come to me, and do not hinder them,
for the kingdom of God belongs to such as these. . . . Anyone who
will not receive the kingdom of God like a little child will never
enter it.' And he took the children in his arms, put his hands on
them and blessed them." *Mark 10:14-16*

Even though Jesus had told the disciples how valuable little children were
to him, how every child's angel has access to the Father's throne, yet Christ's
first kindergarten class was almost sent away from Jesus by his well-meaning
friends. Jesus said, "Stop sending them away. The kingdom belongs to little
children."

Wouldn't we have enjoyed crowding near him with our babies, hearing
his soft voice call them by name, watching him caress them? What Jesus said
to the children we do not know, but we can be sure he neither talked down to
them nor did he speak above their heads. I like to picture Christ smiling with
the children; he did not tease them nor laugh at them as some people are in-
clined to do. Taking them up in his arms, he simply loved them, laying the
same kind hand on their heads that had brought strength and healing to so
many.

Most parents are eager to bring their children to Jesus. But how often do
their own hearts crave his fellowship? It has been said that little children
respond more easily to Christian teaching than older people because of their
rare combination of curiosity and confidence, their eagerness to learn and their
willingness to believe.

Are we as mothers also ready to sit at the feet of Jesus, drinking in his life-
giving words along with our children? We can keep on learning about God and
God's creation as we teach our children. While we watch God bless our babies,
we, too, can worship and be blest.

*Just as the mothers long ago, dear Christ, brought their little ones to you
for your blessing, so I bring my baby to you today. Take my child up in your
everlasting arms to love and to bless. And help me always to come to you for
blessing and inspiration. In your name I ask these special favors. Amen.*

39

HE TEACHES YOU

He's greater far, that little child, than you;
The very child you teach, he teaches you.
  You teach him to be Christlike, but have you
  Forgotten he already is, far more than you?
  You teach him right from wrong, and yet it's he,
  Not you, whose conscience is more clear and free.
  You teach him trust in God, but can't you see
  That it is you who lack trust more than he?
  For you find doubt and reason in your way
  While he in simple faith believes straightway.
  You teach him to forgive, but don't you know
  That he forgives in half the time you do?
  And he, when he forgives, at once forgets;
  But you? You struggle long with grudge and debts.
  You try to teach him love. You can't. You cry,
  "My child, you are the teacher, and not I!"
So learn from him, be like him, you who teach.
You must, Christ says, if heaven you would reach.

Ida Boyer Bontrager

The Child Teaches Us Humility

"Therefore, whoever humbles himself like this child is the greatest in the kingdom of heaven."
Matthew 18:4

If you, a daughter of the King, would be truly humble, consider the baby which God has given you!

Paul once said to Timothy, "For we brought nothing into this world, and it is certain we can carry nothing out." If ever anyone came to your house with an empty suitcase, your baby did. Aside from those personality and physical and mental capacities waiting to be developed, your baby came to this world empty-handed.

The infant comes without ambition or reputation. Indeed, young children can afford to be themselves at all times; they need never put up a front. That word "innocence" describes how completely without worldly wisdom your little one is.

Your baby entered this world without a resentment of any kind, and it will be a long time before the child learns to hold a grudge or carry ill will around on little shoulders. Would to God that no child would ever learn that. A twig unbent, totally bereft of any prejudices, humble, sincere, and a learner, the child is utterly teachable.

The baby enters this universe without anxiety. If your child has any "fears" at all, they are not the foolish, complicated variety that haunt our grown-up lives. The baby is not troubled about where the next meal will come from nor what will happen tomorrow.

Probably the outstanding lesson Jesus wanted us to learn from the child is the lesson of *humility*, fundamental to all the other Christian graces.

To humble ourselves as a little child, we must lay aside ambition and reputation, resentments and prejudices, anxieties and materialistic concerns of this life. Stripped of the veneer of sophistication which hides our genuine selves, we must let the honest, sincere, trustful, loving and forgiving, learning child live within us. For "anyone who will not receive the kingdom of God like a little child will never enter it."

I praise you, Father, Lord of heaven and earth, because you have hidden these things from the wise and learned, and revealed them to little children. (A prayer of Jesus as recorded in Matthew 11:25.)

41

TRUST IN GOD

The child leans on its parent's breast,
Leaves there its cares and is at rest;
The bird sits singing by his nest,
*   And tells aloud*
His trust in God, and so is blest
*   'Neath every cloud.*

He has no store, he sows no seed;
Yet sings aloud, and doth not heed;
By flowing stream or grassy mead,
*   He sings to shame*
Men, who forget, in fear of need,
*   A Father's name.*

The heart that trusts for ever sings,
And feels as light as it had wings;
A well of peace within it springs;
*   Come good or ill.*
Whate'er today, tomorrow, brings,
*   It is his will.*

Isaac Williams

42

The Child Teaches Us Trust

"If you, then, though you are evil, know how to give good gifts
to your children, how much more will your Father in heaven give
good gifts to those who ask him!"

Matthew 7:11

Read Matthew 7:7-11

When my first child was born and I saw how completely helpless and dependent he was upon me, I was frightened, for I knew my own limitations and lack of experience. It was fortunate that the baby was ignorant of mother's woeful inexperience: otherwise he never would have slept so sweetly in his little basket!

The utter dependence of a new baby upon mother has often been used to illustrate the helpless state in which we find ourselves, as children of our God in heaven. Just as a mother watches over her child with unfailing love, regardless of the child's inability to express needs in words and sentences, so the loving heart of God is sensitive to our every cry. Our Father knows what things we have need of even before we ask, as Jesus assured his disciples.

As a child grows older, trust in parents becomes a more intelligent response to love expressed in many little ways. Despite a painful trip to the dentist, a dose of foul-tasting medicine, or an occasional spanking, the child experiences our genuine love.

Sometimes we as Christians are faced with situations which try us and for which we, like Job, can see no reason. Our trust in God, to be really perfect and childlike, must accept the higher wisdom of God's love in difficult situations as well as when things are going our way. Paul's advice to the Philippians on prayerful trust is "good for what ails us" today. Let's put it to practice!

"Do not be anxious about anything, but in everything, by prayer and petition, with thanksgiving, present your requests to God. And the peace of God, which transcends all understanding, will guard your hearts and your minds in Christ Jesus" (Philippians 4:6-7).

My loving Father in heaven, how glad I am that I can relax in the thought of your tender concern for me. Just as my baby trusts in me completely, so I rest in the security of your love. Give me the inner peace that manifests itself in strength and poise. In the name of your Son I ask this. Amen.

SAVIOR, TEACH ME DAY BY DAY

Savior, teach me day by day
Love's sweet lesson to obey;
Sweeter lesson cannot be:
Loving him who first loved me.

With a childlike heart of love,
At thy bidding may I move,
Prompt to serve and follow thee—
Loving him who first loved me.

Jane E. Leeson

The Child Teaches Us the Love of God

"As a mother comforts her child, so will I comfort you."
Isaiah 66:13

"As a father has compassion on his children, so the Lord has compassion on those who fear him."
Psalm 103:13

A young mother, noticing that the baby of the family was not benefiting from her Bible story hour with the older children, decided that she would show her the love of the heavenly Father in a more understandable way—by taking her in her arms and rocking her gently. As she sat thus meditating and cuddling her baby, her own spiritual life was enriched and strengthened.

A dear disciple of Christ, eighty-nine years of age, once said that although he was the fifteenth child in his family, he always believed that his mother loved him best of all. During the many years that followed his babyhood, the memory of that loving Christian mother pointed him to a God who comforts like a mother and has compassion as an earthly father.

As much as we love our babies, we know that God loves us with a more perfect love. We are such imperfect symbols of God's parental affection. Our heavenly parent is never annoyed when we cry, is never physically tired, never slumbers nor sleeps, but watches over us with even deeper concern than we have for our own little sleepers. How warm, how secure, how comforting it is to have a God like that!

One evening, as I sat feeding my baby, he suddenly stopped eating, laid his head against my shoulder, and patted my face, blissfully cooing, "Ahhh, Ahhh." As I pondered this little note of endearment, I came to the conclusion that true worship is probably nothing more than touching the kind cheek of the heavenly Father and whispering, "Ahhh, Ahhh, dear Father."

Oh, that my worship of you, dear God, would be as free and spontaneous as the love of a little child for her mother. Help me to nurture my babe in such a tender way that when we talk about your love, the growing child will understand and love you in response. Amen.

FAITH OF OUR MOTHERS

Faith of our mothers, living yet
In cradle song and bedtime prayer,
In nursery love and fireside lore,
Thy presence still pervades the air.
Faith of our mothers, living faith,
We will be true to thee till death.

Faith of our mothers, lavish faith,
The fount of childhood's trust and grace,
O may thy consecration prove
The wellspring of a nobler race.
Faith of our mothers, lavish faith,
We will be true to thee till death.

Faith of our mothers, guiding faith,
For youthful longings—youthful doubts,
How blurred our vision, blind our way,
Thy providential care without.
Faith of our mothers, guiding faith,
We will be true to thee till death.

Faith of our mothers, Christian faith,
In truth beyond our man-made creeds,
Still serve the home and save the church,
And breathe thy spirit through our deeds.
Faith of our mothers, Christian faith,
We will be true to thee till death.

Arthur B. Patten

The Child, Our Imitator

"I have been reminded of your sincere faith, which first lived in your grandmother Lois and in your mother Eunice and, I am persuaded, now lives in you also."

2 Timothy 1:5

"When I grow up I want to be just like Mother (or Daddy)," is a more sobering statement than we perhaps think. For children are little imitators, every one of them, and they are going to imitate and grow to be like those with whom they live. The story is told of a little girl who was heard screeching at her dolls. When her mother asked the reason, she replied that she was playing "Mamma."

There are many vital habits which the child picks up unconsciously from parents—little mannerisms, polite or rude manners, a sunny or a grouchy disposition, neat or slovenly appearance, good or bad attitudes, words, and actions.

Seeing one's personal faults and virtues in one's children has a rather startling effect on the average parent. Joseph Joubert, in 1842, expressed a great truth when he said, "Children need models more than they need critics." Children are quick to notice if we preach one thing and practice another. Nor can we hide unkind attitudes or other inconsistencies, thinking that our children will not see our real selves.

The apostle Paul said, "Follow my example, as I follow the example of Christ." Can we sincerely ask our little ones to follow us as *we* follow Christ? Are we passing on to them our strong faith, evident in our every word and action?

> I tried to lead a child through play
> To grow more Christlike every day
> And I myself became that way.
>
> *Mabel Niedermeyer McCaw*

Dear Christ, this tiny baby, now so unconscious of all that is going on in our household, will soon be watching and imitating the things I do. May I so closely imitate you that I will not need to fear my influence on this young life. Mold me, O Christ, to your own image, that my children may see the beauty of Jesus in me. Amen.

I WOULD BE TRUE

I would be true, for there are those who trust me;
 I would be pure, for there are those who care;
I would be strong, for there is much to suffer;
 I would be brave, for there is much to dare.

I would be friend of all—the foe, the friendless;
 I would be giving, and forget the gift;
I would be humble, for I know my weakness;
 I would look up, and live, and love, and lift.

Howard Arnold Walter

The Child, Our Challenge to Pure Living

"Create in me a pure heart, O God, and renew a steadfast spirit within me." *Psalm 51:10*

Have you ever cuddled your baby to your breast and said, perhaps not aloud, "You dear, innocent little soul, what a wretched old world I've brought you into"? I have done this. But I've gotten over worrying about what will become of my children in the far-flung years of the future. For the most formative period of their lives are those years with me before they ever face that dubious, unreliable character, John Q. Public.

While my small children are still tagging on to the hem of my garment, they are going to be getting their basic training in life. As we noticed yesterday, they are going to imitate me, to gradually absorb my actions and reactions, my habits and attitudes. This calls for scrupulous self-examination on my part and daily cleansing at the cross of Christ. What a challenge to pure living is the unstained life of a little child!

But how do we fit the devotional life into our busy mother schedules? When we are consciously walking with God, we are surprised at our many opportunities for informal fellowship with the Lord. Those pleasant periods when nursing or rocking our babies can well be used for meditation on a spiritual truth we need at the moment, for give-and-take conversation with the Lord, for thanksgiving and praise. We can memorize hymns as we fold clothes. We can paste a precious Scripture above the kitchen sink. We can bring such big-little things to God as the formula we are mixing or the baby's colic.

The unblemished life of a newborn baby does indeed have a purifying influence on the lives of Christian parents. And it is only by keeping our own hearts and minds centered on the Lord Jesus Christ, that we will be able to lead our children into "whatever is true ... noble ... right ... pure ... lovely ... admirable" (Philippians 4:8).

Dear Jesus, thank you that you are interested in every detail of my life. Help me to worship you as I go about my daily routine. Give me the grace to live above petty irritations and fretful worries. And when I fail, create in me a clean heart, O God, and renew a right spirit within me. Amen.

TIME-HONORED TRUTH

The statement may seem very trite—
It has been said so often,
That babies have been sent from heav'n
Our calloused hearts to soften.

But though the story may be old,
It's changed no jot or tittle;
The baby is God's messenger
E'en though he is so little.

And so I feel the aged truth
Needs no fresh interpretation—
A baby's face is heaven's grace
To any generation.

Helen Good Brenneman

The Child, Preserver of Life Values

"Listen, my sons, to a father's instructions;
   pay attention and gain understanding.
I give you sound learning,
   so do not forsake my teaching.
When I was a boy in my father's house,
   still tender, and an only child of my mother,
he taught me and said,
   'Lay hold of my words with all your heart;
   keep my commands and you will live.' "

Proverbs 4:1-4

In the days when the great-grandchildren of the aged Joseph were brought to his knees to be blessed, people considered it a high privilege to become acquainted with and to influence one's posterity. In Psalm 128:6 we read, "May you live to see your children's children. Peace be upon [your people]." This promise may be claimed by everyone who fears the Lord. Proverbs 17:6 states, "Children's children are a crown to the aged, and parents are the pride of their children."

One day my husband and I were invited as guests to a large family reunion. The carry-in dinner was spread on long tables; the picnic grounds were dotted with cousins of every age and size. To our surprise we were informed that all these people, despite their differences in personality and appearance, were by birth or marriage direct descendants of one couple just a few generations back.

We could only wonder what a family reunion several years hence would reveal in our own children and our children's children. Will our Christian nurture be strong and winsome enough to bear fruit in future generations? What ideals will we plant in our young, what values will we teach as important?

In our children we have an opportunity to live again, for the child is a preserver of our values. Thus may we strive for the highest goals in life, as did one minister who said, "If we cannot leave a single dollar to our children, let us give them the more important heritage of godly Christian parents."

Thank you for strong family ties that bind us together with those we love. Thank you for my own parents and grandparents who taught me principles of right living. Bless the baby's grandparents, give wisdom to us the parents, and help us all to inspire our little one to love and follow you. Amen.

INNER TRIUMPH

Not in the clamor of the crowded street,
Not in the shouts and plaudits of the throng,
But in ourselves are triumph and defeat.

Henry Wadsworth Longfellow

"A man who controls his temper [is better] than one who takes a city."

Proverbs 16:32

The Child, an Individual

"And the Lord God formed man from the dust of the ground
and breathed into his nostrils the breath of life, and man became a
living being."   ***Genesis 2:7***

Before we close this section of meditations on the child and the child's significance for us, we must consider each baby as a new and separate individual. Though the newborn may look like Uncle John and have ears like the mother's side of the family, God has given each an individual personality, one which like a bud will gradually unfold before our wondering eyes.

Alta Mae Erb, in her book on *The Christian Nurture of Children*, says that a child's personality is determined by: inherited possibilities, physical body, surroundings, an individual self, and salvation of this self through Christ. And strange as it may seem, the first six months of an infant's life are very significant, for the many influences on a child's personality begin operating powerfully when still a babe-in-arms.

To ignore the rights of a little child as a person is unkind and unjust. Children are not grownups in miniature form and dare not be treated as such. Their personalities need to be respected, and we need to build solid character and lofty ideals upon each one's own particular characteristics and needs. Although we cannot preach sermons to a baby who is only three weeks old, we can start developing the text of our lifetime sermon: love. For the love of two emotionally mature Christian parents is our baby's greatest need.

Delicate plants require patient, skillful, loving care. How much more does the sensitive personality of a little child need the sunshine of our love and the careful nurture of sympathizing parents. What a privilege and what a *responsibility* it is for us to guard the development of an immortal soul!

Dear God, in view of all that is expected of a mother, I would feel most inadequate were not my hand in yours. I thank you for entrusting me with a living soul. Help me to bring out the best that is in my child by teaching that above all things we are to live, move, and have our being in you. In Jesus' name. Amen.

THE CHILD'S APPEAL

I am the Child.
All the world waits for my coming.
All the earth watches with interest to see what I shall become.
Civilization hangs in the balance,
For what I am, the world of tomorrow will be.

I am the Child.
I have come into your world, about which I know nothing.
Why I came I know not;
How I came I know not.
I am curious; I am interested.

I am the Child.
You hold in your hand my destiny.
You determine, largely, whether I shall succeed or fail.
Give me, I pray you, those things that make for happiness.
Train me, I beg you, that I may be a blessing to the world.

Mamie Gene Cole

The Child, Our Trust

"So then, no more boasting.... All things are yours ... the
world or life or death or the present or the future—all are yours."
1 Corinthians 3:21-22

Of all the challenging truths which we, like Mary, have pondered in our hearts since our baby's birth, our small part in creating an everlasting soul is surely the most awe-inspiring. Masefield states the majesty of giving birth to a child in the words:

"And he who gives a child a treat
Makes joy-bells ring in Heaven's street,
And he who gives a child a home
Builds palaces in Kingdom come,
And she who gives a baby birth
Brings Savior Christ again to Earth."°

One evening my husband and I called in the home of new parents and found them sitting blissfully in their living room, watching the sleeping infant with quiet satisfaction. "Such a sweet little life God has given us to care for," the mother whispered. "Just think, our baby is really not ours, but God's."

I like to think of the security of a baby born in a Christian home. In a way, we can call the baby our own, but since we are Christ's and Christ is God's, the baby ultimately belongs to God. How secure our children are in the close relationship of God's "family tree."

Thus, as we meditate upon our child, we realize this little one is given us in stewardship and trust, to raise and nurture for God. Like the mother of Samson we cry at this point, "Teach us how to bring up the [child]...." And how ready our heavenly teacher is to do just that!

Lord, I gladly accept this trust which you have given me. I thank you for the lovely dependence of a baby upon parents, of one parent upon the other, and of both parents upon you. Therefore I do not take the responsibilities of motherhood upon my own shoulders alone. In you I go forward with confidence. Amen.

° John Masefield, *The Everlasting Mercy*

Our Responsibility to the Child

"So now I give him to the Lord."
1 Samuel 1:28

FOR MATTHEW

Dear Little One,
Our newest, tenderest son,
What world we brought you to, we cannot know.

Neither did Hannah know
As on her happy heart sweet Samuel lay
A very Yes of God.

Neither did Eunice know
As, prattling prayers, the tiny Timothy stood
Within her circling arms.

Nor did the saintly Monica foresee
If her Augustine's world should thrive or split;

And that unique Susannah, tutoring
Young John, small Charles,
She knew no more than they ...

Than I. But I do know,
As faith-filled they too knew,
That if your times be anguished or be still
It is God's will
That you should live therein to his high praise.

And so I singing hold you to myself.
In strong sweet faith I sing;
Our little son,
Dear, newest, tenderest one.

Miriam Sieber Lind

58

Dedicating and Educating

"So now I give him to the Lord."
1 Samuel 1:28

We all admire the woman Hannah, who prayed for Samuel, thanked God for his coming, and dedicated him to Jehovah, making what seems to us a supreme sacrifice. At the same time we wonder what we have in common with her experience, for we continue to bear responsibility for our children, do we not? We do not take them to a temple and give them to an old man to take care of. That was what God asked of Hannah, but he asks us not only to *dedicate* but also to *educate* our children.

Exactly how long Hannah had her son with her we do not know, but women those days did not wean their children as early as we do now. On the basis of Jewish customs some Bible students believe that she took Samuel to the temple only for a visit during his infancy and then left him there when he was six years old. Be that as it may, after she had placed his dimpled hand in the wrinkled one of Eli, Hannah's task was done, except for her trip each year to take him the new coat she had made so carefully for him.

There probably isn't one of us who would want to trade places with Hannah. Yet, when we dedicate our babies to the Lord we, too, make a sobering commitment. As God leaves them in our care we will lead them in the way of righteousness trusting that they will sometime dedicate their *own* young lives to God's service.

Knowing the one to whom we dedicate, however, takes away any haunting dread of releasing to God what seems to be ours. And to know the Shepherd who "gathers the lambs in his arms and carries them close to his heart" (Isaiah 40:11) sets us free from those foolish worries that ordinarily trouble us. It is in dedication that we, like Hannah, find a new and triumphant peace.

Since you, dear God, gave us your only Son, in perfect love, I gladly dedicate my child to you. Work out your plan for my child's life. And with this dedication I surrender any anxious thoughts, conscious or subconscious, concerning my baby's health, safety, and future. In the name of Jesus. Amen.

THE HOUSEWIFE

Jesus, teach me how to be
Proud of my simplicity.

Sweep the floors, wash the clothes,
Gather for each vase a rose.

Iron and mend a tiny frock
Taking notice of the clock,

Always having time kept free
For childish questions asked of me.

Grant me wisdom Mary had
When she taught her little Lad.

Catherine Cate Coblentz

Our Child's Physical Care

"And if anyone gives a cup of cold water to one of these little
ones because he is my disciple, I tell you the truth, he will certainly
not lose his reward." **Matthew 10:42**

One of the hardest things to understand is how God can, on one hand, rule the universe in infinite power, and at the same time keep an accurate record of the number of hairs on our head. Since our finite minds cannot grasp such a complex system of eternal bookkeeping, we of little faith find it difficult to believe that we shall be rewarded for so small a service as a cup of cold water given in the name of Jesus.

Have you ever wondered how far around the world a two-year diaper wash would go, if all the diapers you launder in that time were hung on a clothesline side by side? Have you ever been tempted to think that you had nothing to show for your day's work after a day in which the baby took more care than usual, perhaps crying a great deal and making extra laundry? If you have ever felt that all the detailed, intimate, time-consuming duties that go with the physical care of a baby are unnoticed by God, then reread Matthew 10:42.

Helping the newborn infant to satisfy biological needs, such as sucking, sleeping, feeling the mother's gentle touch is an important part of mothering. We are told that the way a mother feeds, washes, or diapers her baby conveys her love and concern even before the baby can understand the meaning of her words. How important, then, it is that we perform these duties in a spirit of love and devotion.

We care for our babies in the name of Christ when we do each little task as for God, putting love into everything we do. We do all our daily work in Christ's name when we seek divine guidance and blessing, even on the smallest duties of our days.

God of grace and God of glory, I never realized how many problems a new mother faces until I became a mother myself. I thank you for the many helpful books on child care and for kind friends and good doctors who are ready to give a word of encouragement and assistance. As I follow my daily schedule of feeding, bathing, diapering, and comforting my baby, may I seek your help in each small task, doing it all with tender care, as for you. Amen.

BABY'S SMILE

The doctors and the nurses state
My baby's smile a fake.
It's not a smile at all, they say—
It's just the tummy ache.

But Grandma's explanation
Is much nicer, far, than this—
An angel stooped from heaven
And gave my babe a kiss.

Helen Good Brenneman

Our Child's Emotional Care

"Then they can train the younger women to love their husbands
and children." ***Titus 2:4***

"Say, Mamma, let's laugh." With these words one little girl told her mother that she needed some fun, a bit of her joyous companionship. Perhaps the mother was very busy at the moment and did not sense that her child felt just a little lonely, that she needed her. Is that not the trouble with us mammas? We are sometimes so busy taking care of our children's physical bodies, that we forget their inner need, their emotional care.

Those who study children tell us that pleasant experiences cause children to develop feelings of love and that "bad" children are often "unhappy" children. Insufficient parental affection is bound to show up in a child's personality and behavior, for little children just do not develop as they should—physically, mentally, or spiritually—when their hunger for love is not satisfied.

One doctor, in speaking of a child's need for love, suggests that a newly born infant responds to physical contact, to caressing, to words of delight, and to prompt attention to physical needs. At all ages the child needs to feel wanted, not so much because of being good but because of being loved.

Although God has bountifully blessed us with a natural love for our babies, we need to learn to express the love meaningfully to the child. Giving intelligent love takes time, thought, and patience, and, like vitamins, is a daily requirement. But the confidence our children have in us, and the companionship they share with us, will be well worth all the time and energy we invest in demonstrating to them how much we love them.

O God, you are love itself, and you have shed light and love into my soul. Only you know how the seams of my heart are bursting with affection for this little mite. Help me to remember that life out in this world is very different from the security and warmth of my body, where the newborn lived for nine months. Help me to hold the baby tenderly, communicating love and acceptance. Amen.

THE TEACHER

Lord, who am I to teach the way
To little children day by day,
So prone myself to go astray?

I teach them knowledge, but I know
How faint the flicker and how low
The candles of my knowledge glow.

I teach them power to will and do,
But only now to learn anew
My own great weakness through and through.

I teach them love for all mankind
And all God's creatures, but I find
My love comes lagging far behind.

Lord, if their guide I still must be,
Oh, let the little children see
The teacher leaning hard on thee.

Leslie Pinckney Hill

64

Our Child's Intellectual Care

"These commandments that I give you today are to be upon
your hearts. Impress them on your children. Talk about them
when you sit at home and when you walk along the road, when
you lie down and when you get up."

Deuteronomy 6:6-7

Do children really learn half of all they will ever know by the time they
are three years old, as some people believe? If that is true, then H. W.
Beecher's statement, "The mother's heart is the child's schoolroom," is a real
challenge to mothers.

What kind of intellectual care will our baby receive while still in our
"schoolroom," long before going to public school? What courses will we teach?
Will the classroom syrroundings (our home) be artistic and teach the meaning
of beauty? Will the "playground equipment" (the toys) teach our child
constructive activity? Will we carefully answer all questions? Will there be
good books and good music to develop early tastes? Most important of all, will
the Bible be the chief book in our library?

Many people think that the public school alone educates their children.
This is a serious mistake. By the time those curls and pigtails bob into a
schoolroom, the children should have completed many courses in Christian living: obedience, respect for parents and teachers, love for others, love for God.
They should have had many other classes, too: handicraft, drawing, music,
home economics. Mother as president, Daddy as dean, and both of them
should have been educating ever since the babies first began to coordinate
mind and muscle in the world's greatest school—the home. Jesus gave us the
goal for Christian education: "Love the Lord your God with all your heart and
with all your soul and with all your strength and with all your *mind.*"

*O Lord, I thank you for the many privileges of playing with my baby,
supplying many worthwhile toys and books and much music; teaching the
many basic lessons of life. May my child learn, while growing older, that you
are the source of all beauty, all knowledge, and all wisdom. This I ask in your
most worthy name. Amen.*

AT FOUR WEEKS

His tiny fists are clenched above his head—
His fair, round face is sweet in infant sleep—
And as I finger fringes of the shawl
That lies so slight and soft against my dress,
I pray for him:
    Lord, may he love this place—
    This house of thine, erected by thy grace
    Where thy dear Word is taught, thy praises sung.
    Oh, true, he is so very, very young
    And he may cry within these walls, or shout
    In happy, babyish mischief, or call out
    To Daddy in the pulpit. True, he may
    Not understand what Daddy has to say—
    The implications of the Trinity
    Or what "atonement" means to him and me.
    It may be, first, that folding hands in prayer
    Is all the fellowship his soul can share.
    But as his Savior grew, oh, may he grow.
    In sure and silent ways, may his heart know
    That thou art here. And may my conduct be
    A commentary on my love to thee—
    An explanation louder than my speech
    To reach where Daddy's sermons may not reach.
The singing is resumed; the Scripture's read . . .
The tiny fists now stir above his head.
A little dream-smile flits across his face.
Oh, may he learn to love this holy place!

Miriam Sieber Lind

66

Our Child's Spiritual Care

"Train a child in the way he should go, and when he is old he
will not turn from it." *Proverbs 22:6*

"Bring them up in the training and instruction of the Lord."
Ephesians 6:4

Jesus often expressed love and respect for little children! On a sacred day
in Peter's life Jesus asked him three times "Do you really love me?" Jesus
charged him first to feed Jesus' lambs, and then he told him to feed Jesus'
sheep. Of every Christian parent Christ expects spiritual care of the little ones.
"Mother, do you really love me? Then feed my lambs."

It matters *what* we feed little lambs. We do not take them out on the
hillside and give them large tufts of stout wire grass. Likewise, a child under-
stands and digests only those spiritual truths which fit into the limited
experience of childhood. We must know God's Word, know our children, and
then adapt our singing and teaching to the understanding of the child.

How we feed the lambs is also important. One well-meaning father
forced his hungry little boy to learn a verse of Scripture every morning before
breakfast. The boy naturally grew to dislike the Bible. Unwise parents have
been known to use Bible reading as punishment for their children. How could
these children grow up to love the Word of God?

The *when* and *where* of lamb feeding is all the time and everywhere.
Robbie Trent, in *Your Child and God*, says, "Shall I teach my child of God? I
am answering that question every day. For good or for ill, positively or nega-
tively, for faith or for fear, I am teaching my child of God."

There will be times when we give our lambs direct nurture: Bible stories,
verses, hymns, and prayers, Sunday-school and church experiences. But the in-
direct nurture of love and faithfulness in all our ways makes the words meaningful when we tell the little ones of their loving heavenly Father.

*Our loving God, we cannot yet teach this tiny child to pray. But help us,
as mother and father, to treat our baby and each other in such a way that when
the child learns to talk with you, there will be an awareness that you are kind
and good and loving and just and forgiving. Amen.*

WHERE DID HE GO?

I'll only have this little boy but once.
Sometimes, a few years hence,
You'll come to visit, and you'll ask,
"Where did that little tousled-headed,
    brown-eyed infant go?"
And I will say,
"I do not really know.
I only know that now a man,
Tall, self-possessed, intelligent,
Is here instead.
But where that scamp'ring little fellow went,
The one who threw my good shoes out the door
And tossed his dinner plate upon the floor
And tore the pages from my best-loved book
And haunted every corner, crevice, nook,
I do not know, I cannot really say
Just where he went, but here to stay
Is this tall lad—
Our little boy in larger garments clad."

Helen Good Brenneman

Sweet childish days, that were as long
    As twenty days are now.

W. Wordsworth

Watching Our Child Grow

"And the child grew and became strong; he was filled with
wisdom, and the grace of God was upon him."
Luke 2:40

A very little boy I once knew came running in to his mother one day, laughing heartily at a joke on an older friend of the family.

"He waved at me. He thought I was Daddy."

And that is how it seemed to the little fellow, less than five years old. To small children the world does not look the same as it does to older people. That is why they are so often misunderstood.

Each stage of a child's life is different, and wonderful! When children are still tiny babies, it sometimes seems that they do something new and startling every day. We need to understand the changes they are making and their special needs at various ages, so that we can more intelligently help them. There is nothing more thrilling than watching them grow, but we dare not simply sit back and watch, for we must direct them in developing their powers to the fullest. We must direct their energies into constructive and worthwhile channels.

Studying the nature of a child will help us to understanding and solve the problems confronting us and our little ones. Reading good books on child development is a wise investment of time and money for any parent. Of course, since doctors and research students who study and write about human development are not always Christian, we must read their books with discretion, remembering that our children can never be really "good" without the help of God.

And what a unique privilege we have, as Christian parents, of going to God's Word for the basic principles in solving all our problems in life! For we want our children, like the little boy Jesus, not only to grow and become strong in spirit, and wisdom, but to experience the grace of God within their lives.

God of all wisdom, we thank you for the changes that time brings upon all of us: for growth of little children, for maturity that comes with the years. We would not have our children remain babes, either physically, emotionally, intellectually, or spiritually. As this infant grows day by day into childhood and adulthood, help me as mother to guide these little feet in the narrow path that leads to life. Amen.

A MOTHER'S PRAYER

Father in heaven, make me wise,
So that my gaze may never meet
A question in my children's eyes.
God keep me always kind and sweet,

And patient, too, before their need;
Let each vexation know its place,
Let gentleness be all my creed,
Let laughter live upon my face!

A mother's day is very long,
There are so many things to do!
But never let me lose my song
Before the hardest day is through.

Margaret E. Sangster

Wisdom for Today

"If any of you lacks wisdom, he should ask God, who gives
generously to all without finding fault, and it will be given to him.
But when he asks, he must believe and not doubt."
James 1:5-6

Oh, for more of the wisdom of Solomon, we cry, looking at the responsibilities placed on our mother shoulders and then at our limitations! How can we lead our little ones in straight paths when we ourselves have so many unsolved problems? We can see the mistakes of others, but how can we be sure that we will not make some which are just as bad, or even worse?

But God whose strength is made perfect in our weakness can use our very mistakes to show us a better way. Even Solomon himself uttered this prayer: "Now, O Lord my God, you have made your servant king in place of my father David. But I am only a little child and do not know how to carry out my duties. . . . So give your servant a discerning heart" (1 Kings 3:7, 9).

God honored Solomon's prayer, and in Ephesians 1:17 we are told that we today will be given "the spirit of wisdom and revelation, so that [we] may know him better." To every believing Christian the Holy Spirit is promised, the Spirit who will lead us into all truth.

"I said to the man who stood at the gate of the years,
  'Give me a light that I may find my way.'
But he replied,
  'Go out into the darkness and put your hand in
    the hand of God.
This will be better than light
And safer than a known way.' "
Author Unknown

God of love, I praise you for the way that you have guided my feet until this day, even though I often plod along in the darkness alone, forgetting your interest in my life. Gladly do I place my hand in yours. Humbly do I ask for your wisdom and your strength. Give therefore your servant a discerning heart. In Jesus' name. Amen.

WHAT GOD HATH PROMISED

God hath not promised
Skies always blue,
Flower-strewn pathways
All our lives through;
God hath not promised
Sun without rain,
Joy without sorrow,
Peace without pain.

But God hath promised
Strength for the day,
Rest for the labor,
Light for the way,
Grace for the trials,
Help from above,
Unfailing sympathy,
Undying love.

Annie Johnson Flint

Strength for Today

"I can do everything through him who gives me strength."
Philippians 4:13

"My grace is sufficient for you, for my power is made
perfect in weakness."
2 Corinthians 12:9

During the early months following the birth of a new baby, we mothers feel like a friend of mind who crossed the Atlantic in a four-motor plane which was operating on only two motors because of engine trouble. Just as her trip, instead of being quick and pleasant, was long and tedious, so the routine work which we usually enjoy becomes somewhat laborious.

But it is important that we accept this fact as a very small inconvenience for so great a gift, that we remember it is only a temporary experience and common to parenting, and that we do not let our spiritual vim and vigor lag with our physical. For it is of spiritual strength that Isaiah writes:

"He gives strength to the weary
   and increases the power of the weak. . . .
But those who hope in the Lord
   will renew their strength.
They will soar on wings like eagles;
   they will run and not grow weary,
   they will walk and not be faint."
Isaiah 40:29, 31.

Let us not, however, waste our energies and our strength and then expect God to renew them. If we are to regain our old vitality, we must observe the laws of health: get plenty of rest, nutritious food, physical and mental exercise. We can serve simple meals, sit down to do some routine chores, lie down with our babies when we nurse them. God promises strength, as well as material blessings, in one-day doses only. If we look to our Guide and use common sense in the use of our limited energies, we can be assured that we will be given "strength for today and bright hope for tomorrow."

O God, I thank you for the power which you give to the faint. I know that it will not be long until I once more can run and not be weary, and walk and not faint. Until then, O Father, teach me to be patient. Give me the grace and wisdom to conserve my energies for the most important tasks. Amen.

THE LORD IS MY SHEPHERD

"The Lord is my shepherd,
I shall lack nothing.

"He makes me lie down in green pastures,
He leads me beside quiet waters,
He restores my soul.
He guides me in the paths of righteousness
for his name's sake.

"Even though I walk through the valley of the shadow of death,
I will fear no evil,
For you are with me;
Your rod and your staff, they comfort me.

"You prepare a table before me
In the presence of my enemies.
You anoint my head with oil;
My cup overflows.

"Surely goodness and love will follow me all the days of my life,
And I will dwell in the house of the Lord forever."

Psalm 23

Courage for Today

"Be strong and courageous.
Do not be terrified; do not be discouraged,
For the Lord your God will be with you wherever you go."
Joshua 1:9

Our Task:
"Bring them up in the training and instruction of the Lord."
Ephesians 6:4

Our Goal:
"Now this is eternal life: that they may know you, the only true God, and
Jesus Christ, whom you have sent."
John 17:3

Our Resources:
"Therefore put on the full armor of God . . .
with the belt of truth buckled around your waist,
with the breastplate of righteousness in place,
and with your feet fitted with the readiness
that comes from the gospel of peace.

"In addition to all this, take up the shield of faith. . . .
Take the helmet of salvation
and the sword of the Spirit, which is the word of God."
Ephesians 6:13-17

Our God:
"Surely I will be with you always, to the very end of the age."
Matthew 28:20

Prayer for Today:
Repeat thoughtfully Psalm 23 from memory or read it aloud from the opposite page.

PRAYER OF SAINT FRANCIS

Lord, make me a channel of thy peace,

That where there is hatred I may bring love,
That where there is wrong I may bring the spirit of forgiveness,
That where there is discord I may bring harmony,
That where there is error I may bring truth,
That where there is doubt I may bring faith,
That where there is despair I may bring hope,
That where there are shadows I may bring light,
That where there is sadness I may bring joy.

Lord, grant that I may seek rather

To comfort than to be comforted,
To understand than to be understood,
To love than to be loved;
                for
It is by giving that one receives,
It is by self-forgetting that one finds,
It is by dying that one awakens to eternal life.

St. Francis of Assisi

The Rewards of Motherhood

> "A wife of noble character who can find?
>   She is worth far more than rubies....
> She speaks with wisdom,
>   and faithful instruction is on her tongue.
> She watches over the affairs of her household....
> Her children arise and call her blessed;
>   her husband also, and he praises her."
>
> *Proverbs 31:10, 26-28*

The account of a woman of noble character in Proverbs 31 anticipates the job description of a modern homemaker. She is indeed a competent, respected professional. Someone who does not understand mothers might be tempted to ask what *she* gets out of it all.

Motherhood, however, does not need to seek rewards. There are ample compensations and many daily "surprise packages." As St. Francis prayed, "It is by giving that one receives ... by self-forgetting that one finds." The writer of Proverbs 31 describes in detail many of the duties of the Christian wife and mother, but a careful reading shows that she is not a slave to be pitied. Here are a few of her rewards:

> Her husband has full confidence in her.
> Her husband is respected [in the community].
> Her children call her blessed.
> Her husband praises her.
> She fully earns her ample rewards.

Of course, we do not work for praise; indeed, if we look for it we shall not find it. Love seeks not its own. Nor do we care for flattery.

Like other human beings, mother needs occasionally to be reassured that she is making her loved ones happy. But her children pay her the highest tribute when they love and serve Jesus Christ who once said of a woman, "She has done what she could."

Prayer for Today:
    Read the prayer of St. Francis of Assisi on the opposite page.

Acknowledgments

The publisher attempted to trace the ownership of all poems and quotations and to secure all necessary permissions from authors or holders of copyrights. Should there be any oversight in making proper acknowledgment, upon notification the publisher will correct such omissions in any future editions of this publication.

For permission to reprint from copyrighted works, the author and publisher are indebted to the sources listed below.

W. W. Coblentz for the poem "The Housewife" by Catherine Cate Coblentz from *Christ and the Fine Arts*, Harper and Brothers (1938).

Macmillan Company for the poem "Everlasting Mercy" from *Poems* by John Masefield, The Macmillan Company.

Cynthia Pearl Maus for the poem "A Mother" Author Unknown from *Christ and the Fine Arts*, Harper and Brothers (1938).

Mabel Niedermeyer McCaw for the poem "I Tried to Lead a Child Through Play."

Moody Press for the passages quoted from *The New Testament*, Tr. Charles B. Williams, Moody Press (1937).

Robbie Trent for a quotation from *Your Child and God* by Robbie Trent, Harper and Brothers (1952).

Charles L. Wallis for the poem "A Mother's Prayer" by Margaret E. Sangster from *Masterpieces of Religious Verse*, Harper and Brothers (1948).

The Author

Born in Harrisonburg, Virginia, Helen Good Brenneman spent her childhood years near Hyattsville, Maryland, a suburb of Washington, D.C. She studied at Eastern Mennonite and Goshen colleges, and worked for four years as a clerk in the U.S. Department of Agriculture.

Always interested in writing, Helen longed as a girl to become a newspaper reporter, but later found herself instead writing articles, stories, women's inspirational talks, and devotional books.

Following her marriage to Virgil Brenneman in 1947, the couple served a year in a refugee camp operated by the Mennonite Central Committee in Gronau, Germany, before going to Goshen, Indiana, where her husband studied for the ministry. They served for ten years in two pastorates, at Iowa City, Iowa, and Goshen, Indiana.

Other books by Mrs. Brenneman are *But Not Forsaken, Meditations for the Expectant Mother,* the January section of *Breaking Bread Together* edited by Elaine Sommer Rich, *My Comforters, The House by the Side of the Road, Ring a Dozen Doorbells, Marriage: Agony and Ecstasy, Learning to Cope,* and *Morning Joy.*